Modern Malware

FOR

DUMMIES®

by Lawrence C. Miller, CISSP

WILEY

John Wiley & Sons, Inc.

Modern Malware For Dummies®
Published by
John Wiley & Sons, Inc.
111 River St.
Hoboken, NJ 07030-5774
www.wiley.com

Copyright © 2012 by John Wiley & Sons, Inc., Hoboken, New Jersey

Published by John Wiley & Sons, Inc., Hoboken, New Jersey

WILEY

Table of Contents

Publisher's Acknowledgments

We're proud of this book and of the people who worked on it. For details on how to create a custom *For Dummies* book for your business or organization, contact info@ dummies.biz. For details on licensing the *For Dummies* brand for products or services, contact BrandedRights&Licenses@Wiley.com.

Some of the people who helped bring this book to market include the following:

Acquisitions, Editorial, and Vertical Websites

Senior Project Editor: Zoë Wykes

Editorial Manager: Rev Mengle

Acquisitions Editor: Amy Fandrei

Business Development Representative: Karen Hattan

Custom Publishing Project Specialist: Michael Sullivan

Composition Services

Senior Project Coordinator: Kristie Rees

Layout and Graphics: Carl Byers

Proofreaders: Rebecca Denoncour, Jessica Kramer

Special Help from Palo Alto Networks: Wade Williamson

Publishing and Editorial for Technology Dummies

    Richard Swadley, Vice President and Executive Group Publisher

    Andy Cummings, Vice President and Publisher

    Mary Bednarek, Executive Director, Acquisitions

    Mary C. Corder, Editorial Director

Publishing and Editorial for Consumer Dummies

    Kathleen Nebenhaus, Vice President and Executive Publisher

Composition Services

    Debbie Stailey, Director of Composition Services

Business Development

    Lisa Coleman, Director, New Market and Brand Development

Introduction

• •

*M*odern malware has transformed into highly sophisticated network applications and has, in the process,
changed the world of enterprise security and how networks
are attacked. These threats are experts at remaining hidden
from traditional security while exhibiting an intelligence,
resiliency, and scale that has never before been seen in malware. Controlling these threats will require multiple security
disciplines. While no single solution will solve the problem of
networked malware on its own, the next-generation firewall
provides the unique visibility and control of, and the true integration of, threat-prevention disciplines needed to find and
stop these threats — both known and unknown.

About This Book

This book provides an in-depth examination of real-world
attacks and modern malware threats, the shortcomings of
legacy security solutions, the capabilities of next-generation
firewalls, and security best practices.

Foolish Assumptions

First and foremost, despite the title of this book, we assume
that you know a little something about network security and
Internet-based threats. We know, it's a bit of an oxymoron,
but "Modern Malware For Geniuses" just isn't that catchy! As
such, this book is written primarily for technical readers who
are evaluating potential new security solutions to address
modern malware threats.

How This Book Is Organized

This book consists of six short chapters and a glossary. Here's a brief look at what awaits you!

Chapter 1: Understanding the Modern Threat Landscape

We begin with some real-world examples of high-profile malware invasions. You also get a glimpse into the psyche of a cybercriminal to understand what motivates such a person, and we walk you through the threat lifecycle — from cradle to . . . well, the enterprise network.

Chapter 2: Defining Modern Malware

In this chapter, we describe the characteristics of modern malware and botnets and dissect some of these evil critters!

Chapter 3: Why Traditional Security Solutions Fail to Control Modern Malware

Chapter 3 explains why legacy port-based firewalls and other security solutions are largely ineffective in the fight against modern malware.

Chapter 4: What the Next-Generation Firewall Brings to the Fight against Malware

Here we take a deep dive into the advanced capabilities and features of the next-generation firewall and lay out a practical methodology to protect your enterprise from malware and botnets.

Chapter 5: Creating Modern Malware Protection Policies

Chapter 5 explains the importance of developing organizational security policies and controls, and how to implement and enforce those policies with a next-generation firewall.

Chapter 6: Ten Best Practices for Controlling Modern Malware

Finally, in that classic *For Dummies* format, we end with a Part of Tens chapter chock full of security best practices!

Glossary

And, just in case you get stumped on a technical term or an acronym here or there, we include a glossary to help you sort through it all.

Icons Used in This Book

Throughout this book, we occasionally use special icons to call attention to important information. You won't see any smiley faces winking at you or any other little emoticons, but you'll definitely want to take note! Here's what you can expect:

This icon points out information that may well be worth committing to your nonvolatile memory, your gray matter, or your noggin' — along with anniversaries and birthdays!

You won't find a map of the human genome or the secret to the blueprints for the next iPhone here (or maybe you will, hmm), but if you seek to attain the seventh level of NERD-vana, perk up! This icon explains the jargon beneath the jargon and is the stuff legends — well, nerds — are made of!

Thank you for reading, hope you enjoy the book, please take care of your writers! Seriously, this icon points out helpful suggestions and useful nuggets of information.

Proceed at your own risk . . . *well, okay* — it's actually nothing *that* hazardous. These useful alerts offer practical advice to help you avoid making potentially costly mistakes.

Where to Go from Here

With our apologies to Lewis Carroll, Alice, and the Cheshire cat:

"Would you tell me, please, which way I ought to go from here?"

"That depends a good deal on where you want to get to," said the Cat — err, the Dummies Man.

"I don't much care where . . .," said Alice.

"Then it doesn't matter which way you go!"

That's certainly true of *Modern Malware For Dummies,* which, like *Alice in Wonderland,* is also destined to become a timeless classic!

If you don't know where you're going, any chapter will get you there — but Chapter 1 might be a good place to start! However, if you see a particular topic that piques your interest, feel free to jump ahead to that chapter. Each chapter is individually wrapped (but not packaged for individual sale) and written to stand on its own, so feel free to start reading anywhere and skip around! Read this book in any order that suits you (though we don't recommend upside down or backwards). We promise you won't get lost falling down the rabbit hole!

Chapter 1

Understanding the Modern Threat Landscape

In This Chapter

▶ Seeing the threat through real-world examples

▶ Understanding how hackers have changed

▶ Dissecting the anatomy of a modern attack

▶ Recognizing opportunities to limit and counter threats

*F*or many years, the security industry was seen as Chicken Little, telling anyone who would listen that "the sky was falling" and that hackers were trying to steal their most precious information. For the most part, that simply wasn't the case. Hackers were largely creatures of opportunity seeking the path of least resistance — if they encountered a secured network, they were likely to move on, looking for a softer target. Today's hackers are highly motivated, professional cyber criminals — often well-funded by criminal organizations or rogue nation-states — that are far more patient and persistent in their efforts to break through an organization's defenses.

In this chapter, you find out why hackers are more dangerous than ever before and explore the modern attack lifecycle.

Malware is malicious software or code that typically damages or disables, takes control of, or steals information from a computer system. Malware broadly includes botnets, viruses, worms, Trojan horses, logic bombs, rootkits, bootkits, backdoors, spyware, and adware.

The State of Today's Intrusions

Today's threats are more sophisticated and equal opportunity than ever before. All types of enterprises and information are being targeted. More and more attacks are increasingly coming to fruition, producing a steady stream of high-profile, sophisticated breaches and intrusions, including

- ✔ **Comodo (business partners).** In March 2011, an intruder compromised a reseller's network (not Comodo's own network) and stole nine digital security certificates that could then be fraudulently issued to impersonate various websites operated by Google, Microsoft, Skype, and Yahoo!, among others. This exposure illustrated the potential for attackers to gain sensitive information indirectly by attacking weak spots in a business's ecosystem.

- ✔ **DigiNotar (intellectual property).** In September 2011, the same attacker that claimed responsibility for the Comodo breach (see previous bullet) took credit for a much larger compromise against DigiNotar that occurred during the summer of 2011. Again, a Certificate Authority (CA) was the target and the attacker was able to generate hundreds of seemingly valid certificates for dozens of popular domains. These fraudulent certificates would enable the attacker to conduct future attacks by posing as a valid website to unsuspecting users. DigiNotar filed bankruptcy just two months after the attack was discovered. This is a profound example of how just a single attack can destroy a company's reputation and viability.

- ✔ **RSA (intellectual property).** In March 2011, RSA Security (a division of the EMC Corporation) was infiltrated by an attacker that sent a phishing e-mail with an attached Microsoft Excel spreadsheet file to several RSA employees. The infected file contained malware that used a zero-day exploit in Adobe Flash software to install a backdoor, establish command and control, and steal passwords and sensitive data.

- ✔ **Epsilon (customer information).** In March 2011, a portion of Epsilon's (an online marketing company) clients' customer database was breached "by an unauthorized entry into Epsilon's e-mail system," exposing customer names and e-mail addresses. This information may enable an attacker to create a very credible spear phishing e-mail campaign.

✔ **Sony PlayStation (credit card data).** In April 2011, hackers breached the Sony PlayStation network, potentially stealing credit card and personal information (including names, birthdates, physical and e-mail addresses, passwords, logins, handles, online IDs, purchase histories, and profile data) of more than 100 million subscribers. The value of the personal information to future criminal acts — both cyber and traditional (such as kidnapping and extortion) — could easily outstrip the value of the stolen credit cards (about $1 USD each on the black market).

✔ **U.S. Senate (political hacktivism).** In June 2011, LulzSec (a loosely organized hacker group) broke into the U.S. Senate website and posted a list of compromised — but not sensitive or classified — files online. Other examples of political hacktivism by various hacker groups include attacks against the U.S. Public Broadcasting Service (PBS), Fox Broadcasting Company, and MasterCard, Visa, and PayPal websites in retaliation for negative coverage or adverse actions against WikiLeaks.

Spear phishing is a targeted phishing campaign that appears more credible to its victims by gathering specific information about the target, and thus has a higher probability of success. A spear phishing e-mail may spoof an organization (such as a financial institution) or individual that the recipient actually knows and does business with, and may contain very specific information (such as the recipient's first name, rather than just an e-mail address).

Spear phishing, and phishing attacks in general, are not always conducted via e-mail. A link is all that is required, such as a link on Facebook or on a message board or a shortened URL on Twitter. These methods are particularly effective in spear phishing because they allow the attacker to gather a great deal of information about the targets and then lure them into dangerous clicks in a place where the users feel comfortable.

Many organizations and individuals have been lulled into a false sense of security by the mistaken belief that the only data an attacker wants to steal — and thus the only data that needs to be protected — is financial data, such as credit card numbers or banking information. But breaches are not limited to financial data — if it's valuable to you or your organization, it's very likely to be valuable to someone else as well!

 As the Epsilon and Comodo examples illustrate, you don't have to have the "crown jewels" in your own network to be a victim. How secure are your partner and reseller networks?

The Changing Face of Hackers

Hackers have evolved from the prototypical "whiz kid" — sequestered in a basement, motivated by notoriety, and fueled by too much carbonated caffeine — into a bona fide cybercriminal, often motivated by significant financial gain and sponsored by nation-states, criminal organizations, or radical political groups. Today's hacker fits the following profile:

- ✔ Has far more resources available to facilitate an attack
- ✔ Has greater technical depth and focus
- ✔ Is well funded
- ✔ Is better organized

Why does this matter? Because a kid in a basement may be able to break into a corporate network, but doesn't necessarily know what to do with, say, RSA source code. On the other hand, a rogue nation-state or criminal organization knows exactly what to do or who to sell stolen intellectual property to on the gray or black market.

Additionally, criminal organizations and nation-states have far greater financial resources than independent hackers. Many criminal hacking operations have been discovered, complete with all the standard appearance of a legitimate business with offices, receptionists, and cubicles full of dutiful hackers. These are criminal enterprises in the truest sense and their reach extends far beyond that of an individual hacker.

 Not only do we face more sophisticated adversaries today, but the types of information of value to them are continually expanding as well. These groups can do interesting things with the most seemingly innocuous bits of information.

The Lifecycle of a Modern Attack

The modern attack strategy has also evolved. Instead of a traditional, direct attack against a high-value server or asset, today's strategy employs a patient, multi-step process that blends exploits, malware, and evasion into a coordinated network attack.

As an example, an attack often begins by simply luring an individual into clicking on an infected link. The resulting page remotely exploits the individual, gains root access on the user's computer, and downloads malware to the user's computer in the background. The malware then acts as a control point inside the network, allowing the attacker to further expand the attack by finding other assets in the internal network, escalating privileges on the infected machine, and/or creating unauthorized administrative accounts — just to name a few tactics.

The key is that instead of malware and network exploits being separate disciplines as they were in the past, they are now integrated into an ongoing process. Malware, which is increasingly customized to avoid detection, provides a remote attacker with a mechanism of persistence, and the network enables the malware to adapt and react to the environment it has infected.

Key components of the modern attack strategy include infection, persistence, communication, and command and control (see Figure 1-1).

Infection

Infection almost always has a social aspect, such as getting users to click on a bad link in a phishing e-mail, luring them to a social networking site, or sending them to a web page with an infected image, for example. Understanding how malware and exploits have become closely interrelated in the modern attack lifecycle is important. Exploits used to be directed at vulnerabilities on servers that were directly targeted. Most exploits today are used to crack a target system to infect it with malware: an exploit is run, causing a buffer overflow, which allows the attacker to gain shell access.

Infection	Persistence	Communication	Command & Control
Phishing (Social)	Rootkits/ Bootkits	Encryption (SSL, SSH, Custom)	Common Apps (Social media, P2P)
Hide Transmission (SSL, IM, P2P)	Backdoor (Poision Ivy)	Proxies, RDP, Application Tunnels	Update Configure Files
Remote Exploit (Shell Access)	Anti-AV (InfectMBR)	Port Evasions (tunnel over open ports)	EXE Updates
Malware Delivery (Drive-by-Download)		Fast Flux (Dynamic DNS)	Backdoors and Proxies

Figure 1-1: Key components and tools in the modern attack strategy.

With shell access, the attacker can deliver pretty much any payload. The first step is to exploit the target, then deliver the malware in the background through the application or connection that is already open. This is known as a *drive-by-download* and is far and away the most common delivery mechanism for modern malware today.

Infection relies heavily on hiding from and evading traditional security solutions. Targeted attacks will often develop new and unique malware that is customized specifically for the target network. This technique allows the attacker to send in malware knowing that it is unlikely to be detected by traditional antivirus tools. Another common way to avoid security is to infect the user over a connection that security can't see into, such as an encrypted channel. Attack transmissions are often obscured in SSL-encrypted (Secure Sockets Layer) traffic or other proprietary encryption used in P2P (peer-to-peer) networking applications and IM (instant messaging), for example.

The trend today is that threats do not necessarily come as an executable attachment in an e-mail. A link is all that is required. This is why social media, webmail, message boards, and microblogging platforms such as Twitter are rapidly becoming favorite infection vectors for attackers.

Persistence

Once a target machine is infected, the attacker needs to ensure *persistence* (the resilience or survivability of the bot). Rootkits and bootkits are commonly installed on compromised machines for this purpose. A *rootkit* is malware that provides privileged (root-level) access to a computer. A *bootkit* is a kernel-mode variant of a rootkit, commonly used to attack computers that are protected by full-disk encryption.

Backdoors enable an attacker to bypass normal authentication procedures to gain access to a compromised system. Backdoors are often installed as failover in case other malware is detected and removed from the system. *Poison Ivy* is one example of a backdoor that was used in the RSA attack (discussed earlier in this chapter).

Finally, anti-AV malware may be installed to disable any legitimately installed antivirus software on the compromised machine, thereby preventing automatic detection and removal of malware that is subsequently installed by the attacker. Many anti-AV programs work by infecting the Master Boot Record (MBR) of a target machine.

Communication

Communication is fundamental to a successful attack. Malware must be able to communicate with other infected systems or controllers to enable command and control, and to extract stolen data from a target system or network.

Attack communications must be stealthy and cannot raise any suspicion on the network. Such traffic is usually obfuscated or hidden through techniques that include

- ✔ **Encryption** with SSL, SSH (Secure Shell), or some other custom application. Proprietary encryption is also commonly used. For example, BitTorrent is known for its use of proprietary encryption and is a favorite hacker tool — both for infection and ongoing command and control.

✔ **Circumvention** via proxies, remote desktop access tools (such as LogMeIn!, RDP, and GoToMyPC), or by tunneling applications within other (allowed) applications or protocols.

✔ **Port evasion** using network anonymizers or port hopping to tunnel over open ports. For example, botnets are notorious for sending command-and-control instructions over IRC (Internet Relay Chat) on nonstandard ports.

✔ **Fast Flux (or Dynamic DNS)** to proxy through multiple infected hosts, reroute traffic, and make it extremely difficult for forensic teams to figure out where the traffic is really going.

Command and control

Command and control rides on top of the communication platform that is established but is really about making sure that the malware or attack is controllable, manageable, and updateable.

Command and control is often accomplished through common applications including webmail, social media, P2P networks, blogs, and message boards. Command-and-control traffic doesn't stand out or raise suspicion, is often encrypted, and frequently makes use of backdoors and proxies.

The Central Role of Malware

Attack techniques have also evolved and malware now plays a central role in the hacker's arsenal and in the lifecycle of an attack. Attackers have developed new methods for delivering malware (such as drive-by-downloads), hiding malware communications (with encryption), and avoiding traditional signature-based detection.

Modern malware is somewhat like the pea in a shell game. A street con running a shell game on the sidewalk lures the mark (or victim) into trying to follow the pea, when actually it's an exercise in sleight of hand (see Figure 1-2).

Similarly, the modern threat lifecycle relies on sleight of hand — how to infect, persist, and communicate without being detected.

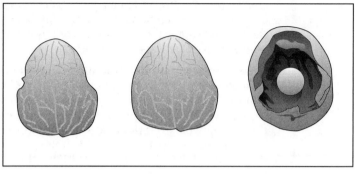

Figure 1-2: The modern threat shell game.

Unfortunately, our traditional view of malware and old security habits make us think of malware as the pea — an executable payload, perhaps attached to an e-mail. To understand, control, and successfully counter modern threats, we need to focus on not just the pea (malware), but on all the moving parts.

We explore the central role of malware in the modern threat lifecycle further in Chapter 2.

Key Security Lessons and Opportunities

For all their sophistication, modern attacks exhibit some vulnerabilities of their own. Some key observations and opportunities to consider include

- ✔ **Communication is the life-blood of an attack.** Modern threats are networked threats that need your network to communicate. If a threat can't communicate, the attack can be largely neutralized.

- ✔ **Numerous opportunities exist to detect and correlate.** By virtue of the fact that multiple steps are involved in the modern attack lifecycle, there are multiple chances to identify and counter threats.

- ✔ **The framework, rather than the functionality, is the threat.** If an attacker can infect targets, persist on, communicate with, and manage bots across the botnet, then the threat functionality can be almost anything. See the threat as an extensible framework, not simply as the functionality of the specific payload.

✔ **Threats exist across multiple disciplines, so too must security.** Firewalls, intrusion prevention, antivirus, content filtering — these security solutions have traditionally been separated to provide "defense in depth." But this strategy makes it difficult — if not impossible — to identify, correlate, and counter complex, coordinated attacks that take advantage of multiple attack vectors, including

- **Applications:** Can hide and enable threats.

- **URLs and websites:** Can host and enable threats.

- **Exploits:** Create shell access to the target.

- **Malware:** controls and uses the compromised target.

- **Files:** Used to update malware and steal data.

✔ **Security must expand beyond the perimeter.** Organizations need to focus on expanding visibility beyond the network perimeter — both inward and outward. This is best accomplished with network segmentation and a next-generation firewall to enforce central controls on internal and external (such as remote and mobile access) network traffic.

The sky is NOT falling! Today's threats are not so advanced that they are impossible to control. They are not completely new, just more common and better organized. Solutions do exist, and organizations can adopt best practices and adapt to changes in the threat landscape. Don't fall into the "APT (Advanced Persistent Threats) ate my homework" trap!

Chapter 2

Defining Modern Malware

● ●

In This Chapter

▶ Understanding how malware became a networked threat

▶ Examining real-world threats to the enterprise

▶ Identifying unique traits of modern malware

● ●

*T*he rise of modern malware is reshaping the threat landscape and forcing enterprises to reassess how they protect themselves. Collectively, modern malware has outpaced traditional anti-malware strategies and in the process, has established a foothold within the enterprise that criminals and nation-states can use to steal information and attack sensitive assets.

In this chapter, you learn about this new class of threat that has come to be known as modern malware — bots, botnets, and bot-herders (but not fem-bots — sorry, Austin Powers!), what makes them tick, and what makes them particularly nasty.

Recognizing Key Characteristics of Modern Malware

Enterprise information security teams have been doing battle with various types of malware for more than two decades. However, all of this hard-earned experience does not mean that enterprises are necessarily winning the war. Recent studies have found reason for concern. A 2009 Cyveillance study (www.cyveillance.com) found that, on average, half of the active malware in the wild was not detected by industry anti-malware solutions, and a 2010 NSS Labs study (www. nsslabs.com) found that only 53 percent of malware was detected on download (see Figure 2-1).

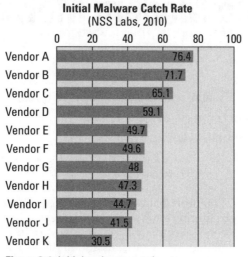

Initial Malware Catch Rate
(NSS Labs, 2010)

Figure 2-1: Initial malware catch rate.

This poor "catch rate" is due to several factors. Some malware has the ability to mutate or can be updated to avoid detection by traditional malware signatures. Additionally, modern malware is increasingly specialized to the point where the attacker will develop a customized piece of malware that is targeted against a specific individual or network.

Botnets are a particularly useful example for understanding some of the unique characteristics of modern malware. *Bots* (individual infected machines) and *botnets* (the broader network of bots working together) are notoriously difficult for traditional antivirus/anti-malware solutions to detect. Bots leverage networks to gain power and resilience. A bot under the remote control of a human attacker (or *bot-herder*) can be updated — just like any other application — so that the attacker can change course and dig deeper into the network, based on what he finds or to adapt to changes and countermeasures.

This is a fundamental shift compared to earlier types of malware, which were more or less a swarm of independent agents that simply infected and replicated themselves. Botnets — and a great deal of modern malware — are centrally coordinated, networked applications in a very real sense. In much the same way that the Internet changed what was possible in personal computing, ubiquitous network access is changing what is possible in the world of malware. Now, all malware of the same type can work together toward a common goal, with each infected machine growing the power and value of the overall botnet. The botnet can evolve to pursue new goals or adapt to changes in security measures.

Some of the most important and unique functional traits of botnets (see Figure 2-2) are discussed in the following sections.

Figure 2-2: Key characteristics of botnets.

Distributed and fault-tolerant

Modern malware takes full advantage of the resiliency built in to the Internet itself. A botnet can have multiple control servers distributed all over the world, with multiple fallback options. Bots can also potentially leverage other infected bots as communication channels, providing them with a near infinite number of communication paths to adapt to changing access options or update their code as needed.

Multifunctional

Updates from the command-and-control servers can also completely change the bots functionality. This multifunctional capability enables a new economic approach for a *bot-herder* (botnet operator), who can now use portions of the botnet for a particular task such as collecting credit card numbers, while other segments of the botnet might be sending spam. The important point is that the infection is the most important step, because the functionality can always be changed later as needed.

Persistent and intelligent

Because bots are both hard to detect and can easily change function, they are particularly well-suited for targeted and long-term intrusions into a network. Since bots are under the control of a remote human bot-herder, a botnet is more like having a malicious hacker inside your network as opposed to a malicious executable program. For example, a bot can be used to learn more about the organization of the network, find targets to exploit, and install additional backdoors into the network in case the bot is ever discovered.

Threats to the Enterprise

Given their flexibility and ability to evade defenses, botnets present an enormous threat to the enterprise. Botnets are virtually unlimited in terms of their functionality — from sending spam to the theft of classified information and trade secrets. The ultimate impact of a botnet is largely left up to the bot-herder: a bot that was sending spam one day could be stealing credit card data the next.

Spamming botnets

The largest botnets are often dedicated to sending spam. The premise is fairly straightforward — the bot-herder infects as many computers as possible, which can then be used without the user's knowledge to send out thousands of spam messages.

Rustock: A real-world example

The *Rustock* botnet is one example of a spamming botnet that operated for at least five years until it was taken down in March 2011. This botnet was capable of sending up to 25,000 spam messages per hour from an individual bot, and at its peak, sent an average of 192 spam e-mails per minute per bot. The Rustock botnet also installed Trojan horses and rootkits on victim machines. It is estimated that as many as 2.4 million computers worldwide were infected.

Microsoft is offering a $250,000 USD reward for information leading to the identification, arrest, and conviction of the individual(s) who were responsible for the Rustock botnet.

DDoS and botnets

A slight twist on the spamming botnet model uses bots as part of a distributed denial-of-service attack (DDoS) — overwhelming a target server or network with traffic from a large number of infected endpoints. In such cases, the enterprise with the infected machine(s) is often not the target of the attack itself. Instead, the infected machine(s) is used to flood some other remote target with traffic. The bot-herder leverages the massive scale of the botnet to generate traffic that overwhelms the network and server resources of the target. DDoS attacks often target specific companies for personal or political reasons, or to extort payment from the target in return for stopping the DDoS attack.

DDoS botnets represent a dual risk for the enterprise. The enterprise itself can potentially be the target of a DDoS attack, resulting in downtime and lost productivity. Even if the enterprise is not the ultimate target, any infected machines participating in the attack will consume valuable network resources and facilitate a criminal act, albeit unwittingly.

The Skunkx bot is a current example of a DDoS botnet. It is capable of performing a variety of DDoS attacks including UDP floods, SYN floods, and HTTP floods and is commonly spread over MSN and Yahoo! Messenger.

Financial botnets

Financial botnets have received widespread coverage in the press, largely due to the spectacular monetary damage they have caused. These botnets are typically not as large and monolithic as spamming botnets, which grow as large as possible for a single bot-herder. Instead, financial botnets are often sold as kits that allow large numbers of attackers to license the code and set about building their own botnets and targets. Even with their smaller size, the impact of these botnets can be enormous. Financial botnets — such as ZeuS and SpyEye — are responsible for the direct theft of funds from all types of enterprises. ZeuS botnets have stolen millions of dollars from numerous enterprises in very short periods of time. Other financial botnets focus on the theft of credit card information or faking ACH bank transfers.

The impact of a financial breach can be enormous for an enterprise. The breach of customer credit card information can lead to serious financial, legal, and brand damage, and the enterprise could lose money that potentially may never be recovered.

Targeted intrusions

Botnets are also a key component of targeted, sophisticated, and ongoing attacks. These types of botnets are very different than their larger brothers. Instead of attempting to infect large numbers of machines to launch malicious large-scale attacks, these smaller botnets aim to compromise specific high-value systems that can be used to further penetrate and intrude into the target network. In these cases, an infected machine can be used to gain access to protected systems and to establish a backdoor into the network in case any part of the intrusion is discovered.

These types of threats are almost always undetectable by antivirus software. They represent one of the most dangerous threats to the enterprise because they specifically target the organization's most valuable information, such as research and development, intellectual property, strategic planning, financial data, and customer information.

Aurora: A real-world example

Aurora is one recent example of a targeted attack that, although considered relatively unsophisticated, nonetheless caused extensive damage and resulted in stolen intellectual property. The attack, targeting approximately 34 organizations including Google, Adobe Systems, Juniper Networks, and Rackspace, began in early 2009 and apparently originated in China. The attack used several variants of various malware and made extensive use of dynamic DNS (DDNS) for command and control.

Botnets: Attack or Defend?

The explosion of botnets has certainly not gone unnoticed in the security industry. Many organizations have teamed up with law enforcement to take action against some of the largest and most notorious botnets. The goal is to separate the bots (the infected machines) from their brain (the command-and-control servers). If the bots can't get to their servers, they can't get new instructions, upload data, or do any of the things that make botnets so dangerous (see Figure 2-3). This "attack" or "top-down" approach is often referred to as a botnet "decapitation" or "takedown." While these takedown efforts are important, they are not practical undertakings for most organizations and should not be confused with or distract security teams from actually protecting an enterprise from modern malware.

The most obvious limitation to this "top-down" approach is that it is incredibly time and resource intensive, and as such, only the largest and most notorious botnets are targeted. As discussed earlier in this chapter, some of the most dangerous types of malware are those used in targeted intrusions, and thus they are not particularly large and are not likely to get widespread attention.

Figure 2-3: A distributed command-and-control infrastructure.

Finally, successfully decapitating or taking down a botnet can take several years. Enterprise security needs are far more immediate — ensuring that an intrusion or exploit does not succeed in the first place (see Figure 2-4). In a very real sense, relying on the security industry to disable a botnet is like waiting for the government to enact a law against an act that someone is committing against you right now.

How the Industry Targets Botnets	How Botnets Target the Enterprise
■ Focus on the largest botnets	■ Small, targeted, customized
■ Focus on spammers	■ Data theft and espionage
■ Years required for remediation	■ Requires immediate remediation

Figure 2-4: Why the top-down model doesn't protect the enterprise.

So while progress has been made attacking botnets at a global level, the simple truth is that the wins provide little solace to an enterprise that is under attack today. This puts the responsibility for protecting the enterprise from botnets squarely on the shoulders of the enterprise itself. In Chapter 3 we discuss what doesn't work, then in Chapter 4 you find out what does work in the fight against modern malware!

Enterprise security teams rarely need to take down an entire botnet at the source. Instead, your security team needs to be more narrowly focused on such things as preventing infections, finding machines that are infected, and limiting the scope of any damage. In short, your goal is not to be Eliot Ness aiming to take down Al Capone, but to be the local beat cop — keeping your community safe from Al Capone's criminal activities.

Analyzing the Indestructible Botnet: TDL-4

In mid-2011, security researchers began tracking a new version of the TDL botnet, which is alternately known as TDSS or Alureon. This new variant — TDL-4 — has built-in mechanisms that protect the botnet from a traditional decapitation takedown, such as Microsoft's takedown against the Rustock botnet in early 2011. These "features" have led some in the security industry to label TDL-4 as "indestructible."

In TDL-4, as with most modern malware, the threat is more about the framework than the actual payload or application.

TDL-4 is primarily spread through affiliates — often pornographic, piracy (software, movie, and music), and video/file sharing websites — that are paid as much as $200 USD for every 1,000 computers that they infect (see Figure 2-5).

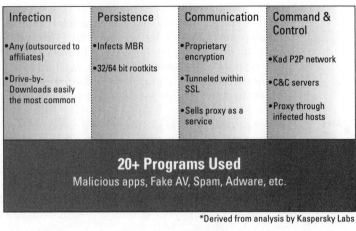

Infection	Persistence	Communication	Command & Control
• Any (outsourced to affiliates) • Drive-by-Downloads easily the most common	• Infects MBR • 32/64 bit rootkits	• Proprietary encryption • Tunneled within SSL • Sells proxy as a service	• Kad P2P network • C&C servers • Proxy through infected hosts

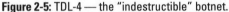

20+ Programs Used
Malicious apps, Fake AV, Spam, Adware, etc.

*Derived from analysis by Kaspersky Labs

Figure 2-5: TDL-4 — the "indestructible" botnet.

Persistence is achieved through installation of a bootkit that infects the Master Boot Record (MBR) of the victim machine, and more than 20 additional malware programs, including fake antivirus programs, adware, and a spamming bot. Very cleverly, TDL-4 actually removes approximately 20 common malware programs — such as Gbot and ZeuS — to avoid drawing unwanted attention to a victim computer when legitimately installed antivirus software detects these common malware programs on the computer!

Communications are concealed using proprietary encryption that is tunneled within SSL. TDL-4 can also install a proxy server on an infected machine, which can then be rented out as an anonymous browsing service that proxies traffic through numerous infected machines. That's right! You're familiar with Software as a Service (SaaS), Infrastructure as a Service (IaaS), and Platform as a Service (PaaS) — get ready for Malware as a Service (MaaS)!

For command and control, TDL-4 uses the Kad P2P network, a publicly accessible P2P file exchange network. TDL-4 updates and distributes information about infected machines over the Kad network, so that even if a command-and-control server is taken down, other infected bots can be found to maintain the botnet — without command-and-control servers.

While all that certainly sounds ominous, there is an important distinction between the way that the security industry goes about completely dismantling a botnet and the steps that an enterprise should undertake to protect itself from that same botnet. A whole host of challenges make botnet takedowns very challenging, not the least of which is the need to take down the entire command-and-control infrastructure in a relatively short window of time. We cover this and other botnet security challenges in the next section.

Modern malware depends on the enterprise network in order to survive. In the truest sense, modern malware consists of networked applications that are uniquely designed to evade traditional security solutions. To detect and stop these threats, security teams need to regain full visibility into network traffic, reduce the exposure of the network and user, and establish new techniques to detect and prevent modern malware. These techniques exist today and are discussed in Chapter 4.

Chapter 3

Why Traditional Security Solutions Fail to Control Modern Malware

• •

In This Chapter

▶ Recognizing the limitations of legacy port-based firewalls

▶ Using social media for work — and for attacks

▶ Exploring the hidden nature of modern malware

▶ Looking at signature detection

▶ Turning to targeted malware

▶ Understanding the need for a fully integrated security solution

• •

*T*oday's application and threat landscape renders traditional port-based firewalls and other security solutions largely ineffective at protecting corporate networks.

In this chapter, you learn how modern malware has challenged these legacy security devices, particularly firewalls, beyond their capability to effectively protect today's networks.

The Rapidly Expanding Attack Surface

In the past, malware was typically delivered over corporate e-mail in the form of attachments or infected documents. This infection method is still used today but is much less prevalent, simply because IT security has become more skilled at protecting corporate e-mail applications.

However, while corporate e-mail applications may be more secure, webmail and other applications are not as secure. In fact, as applications have evolved, literally hundreds of applications have gained the ability to transfer files and content, including

✔ Instant messaging

✔ Webmail

✔ Social media platforms

✔ Microblogging

✔ Workflow and collaboration applications

This means that attackers have far more tools for delivering malware today. To make matters worse, these applications often operate on a real-time model. Hardly anyone notices e-mail delays as messages are inspected for malware on an e-mail server prior to delivery. But now threats are streamed using browsers and any number of other application platforms that, if delayed, will elicit widespread complaints from users.

Unintended Consequences of Social Media

The Internet has spawned a new generation of social media applications that are being accessed by network users for both personal and business use. Many of these applications help improve user and business productivity, while other applications consume large amounts of bandwidth, pose needless security risks, and increase business liabilities. These applications are rapidly becoming a model for future applications. The ability to integrate and interact by using applications that are hosted entirely on the Internet is becoming the dominant model. As such, it is critical for businesses to learn how to manage these applications in a way that captures the benefits while controlling the risks.

The explosive growth of social media in the corporate network is accompanied by explosive growth in the business and security risks associated with these applications. The business risks include what employees can and should post or say about themselves, the projects they work on, and the company. The security risks in social media applications include social engineering and malware delivery.

A Lack of Visibility

In order to maximize their accessibility and use, many applications are designed from the outset to circumvent traditional port-based firewalls by dynamically adjusting how they communicate — and malware threats are coming along for the ride. Simply stated, you can't control threats that you can't see. Modern malware uses various techniques to hide its true nature or existence on the network, including

- ✔ **Nonstandard ports and port hopping.** Evasive applications are one of the key factors leading to the demise of traditional port-based firewalls. These applications merely bypass the simplistic controls defined by ports: If a default port is blocked, they find another port that is open. Most applications do this simply for convenience and ease of use. However, this same tactic is ideal for an attacker wanting to sneak malware or command and control traffic across the network perimeter — in this case, for expressly criminal purposes.

- ✔ **SSL encryption.** Malware creators rely heavily on various forms of encryption to hide infecting traffic, as well as the ongoing command-and-control traffic associated with botnets. SSL is a favorite, simply because it has become a default protocol for so many social media sites, such as Gmail and Facebook. These sites are coincidentally very fertile ground for social engineering and malware delivery. As a result of SSL encryption, many IT security teams lack the ability to see malware traffic on their network. Other types of encryption have also become popular for hiding malware traffic. Peer-to-peer applications provide both infection and command-and-control capabilities, and often use proprietary encryption, again allowing malicious content to pass through the traditional network perimeter undetected.

✔ **Tunneling.** Tunneling provides yet another tool for attackers to hide malicious traffic. Many applications and protocols support the ability to tunnel other applications and protocols within them. This lets attackers disguise their communications as allowed services or applications to get past traditional perimeter security solutions.

✔ **Proxies.** Modern malware and hackers use proxies to traverse traditional firewalls. TDL-4, the "indestructible botnet" (refer to Chapter 2) installs a proxy server on every host that it infects. This allows the bot to not only protect its own communications, but also establishes an anonymous network that anyone can use to hide his tracks while hacking or conducting other illegal activities.

✔ **Anonymizers and circumventors.** Tools such as UltraSurf, Tor, and Hamachi are purpose-built to avoid network security controls. Unlike most of the other technologies discussed in this section, circumventors have almost no legitimate use in an enterprise network. These applications are updated on a monthly (and even weekly) basis to avoid detection in a perpetual cat-and-mouse game with traditional security solutions.

✔ **Encoding and obfuscation.** Malware almost always encodes transmissions in unique ways. Encoding and obfuscation not only help them avoid detection signatures, but also hide the true goal of the malware. This technique can be as simple as converting strings to hexadecimal, or as sophisticated as developing custom algorithms for detailed translations.

Botnets often communicate using Internet Relay Chat (IRC) over nonstandard ports to evade detection.

Finally, many new business applications also use these same techniques to facilitate ease of operation while minimizing disruptions for customers, partners, and the organization's own security and operations departments. For example, RPC (remote procedure calls) and SharePoint use port hopping because it is critical to how the protocol or application (respectively) functions, rather than as a means to evade detection or enhance accessibility.

Fighting blind: The convergence of social media, SSL, and advanced threats

Social media is a well-established hub for social engineering, malware infection, and command and control. This broad category of applications includes social networking, web-based e-mail, instant messaging, web-based file transfer, and a variety of blogs, message boards, and microblogging platforms such as Twitter.

As a group, these applications have become favorite targets for hackers because they provide easy, largely uncontrolled access to the weakest link in enterprise security — the end user. In particular, these applications provide many opportunities to gain the trust of a target user and offer a wealth of links, scripts, ads, and images, all of which can be used to exploit an unsuspecting user. Additionally, the very popularity of these applications makes it easy for an attacker's traffic to blend in with normal user traffic and traverse the network without suspicion. This characteristic is true for outbound as well as inbound traffic, with a variety of bots and malware being known to use social networking, micro-blogging, and message boards as command-and-control channels for the management of a botnet or an ongoing intrusion.

In an effort to improve privacy for their users, many of these applications have begun to use SSL as a default protection for all traffic. This move to SSL has ironically taken a bad security situation and made it worse by encrypting the very channels that hackers are using to attack the network. Now, instead of trying to hide in plain sight or being forced to use a circumventor application that may draw unwanted attention, the attackers can simply ride within the SSL connection between application and the target user. This provides a near-perfect platform for an attacker with a wealth of targets, a full complement of attack vectors, and built-in cloaking from security solutions.

Signature Avoidance

The traditional approach to detecting and blocking malware is based on the simple notion of collecting samples of malware and then writing a signature for that sample. Even at its best, this approach has several drawbacks simply due to the reactive nature of the strategy.

By design, protection can't be delivered until the malware is already "in the wild," during which time networks are blind to the threat. A sample of new or unknown suspicious traffic must be captured and identified before a detection signature can be created by security vendors, in order to provide protection for enterprise networks. This means that some users and networks will be successfully breached by new malware until a new detection signature is created and downloaded. This reactive model creates a window of opportunity for attackers, leaving enterprise networks vulnerable — sometimes for weeks or even months — until new malware is suspected, collected, analyzed, and identified. During this time, attackers have free reign to infect networks and users.

Modern malware has taken this weakness and expanded upon it, by evolving techniques to avoid being captured in the wild and to avoid the signatures that have already been created. Targeted malware and polymorphism, discussed in the next sections, are increasingly common techniques used to exploit the inherent weaknesses of signature-based detection.

Targeted Malware

Before malware became a networked threat, the main goal was often to replicate and spread the malware as widely as possible. In fact, this is how the security industry ranked malware for many years — how many machines could the malware infect in a certain period of time. This widespread replication made new malware samples readily available and relatively easy to collect.

 Modern malware has changed that model, however. Modern malware is more intelligent and highly networked, which enables an attacker to remotely control the target user or users. For savvy attackers, this means that they no longer need millions of infected users. Depending on the goal of the attack, even a single infected host may be enough for a skilled attacker to perform a very sophisticated attack.

In such cases, attackers have increasingly turned to highly targeted malware. These types of malware are often specifically designed for a particular user or network. Stuxnet is an example of targeted malware. It is designed to run only in a specific network with specific assets on the network. This approach accomplishes two very important things. First, it makes it extremely unlikely that a sample of the malware will be captured in the wild, since there are only a few samples instead of millions to be caught. Second, it is designed to avoid infecting networks that are not the intended target, and thereby avoids drawing unwanted attention to itself. This targeted approach is rapidly becoming a hallmark of some of the world's most sophisticated network attacks targeting intellectual property.

Polymorphism

Polymorphism has been used by malware for some time, but continues to be popular today. This approach aims to avoid signatures by regularly mutating to avoid simple signature matches. Some malware applications have entire sections of code that serve no purpose other than to change the signature of the malware.

Traditional Network Controls Are Ineffective

Traditional network security solutions simply were never designed to meet the challenges of modern malware. Traditional firewalls and IPS solutions classify traffic, a firewall allows or blocks traffic, and an IPS determines which signatures to apply, all based on port. As a result, a threat that is evasive and dynamic, such as modern malware, can simply bounce to an unexpected port, gain access to the network, and avoid detection.

Firewalls

Port-based firewalls are often used as a first line of defense, providing coarse filtering of traffic and segmenting the network into different password-protected zones. One drawback to port-based firewalls is that they use protocol and port to identify and control what gets in and out of the network. This port-centric design is ineffective when faced with malware and evasive applications that hop from port to port until they find an open connection to the network. Additionally, firewalls themselves have little ability to identify and control malware.

Solutions that have added anti-malware capabilities to port-based firewalls either as a blade module or as a UTM (Unified Threat Management) platform have typically suffered from poor accuracy and severe performance degradation.

Intrusion prevention

Intrusion prevention systems (IPS) provide a step in the right direction, in that they look much deeper into the traffic than a firewall does. However, IPS solutions typically don't run a complete set of IPS signatures against all traffic. Rather, the IPS attempts to apply the appropriate signatures to specific types of traffic, based on port. This limitation means that malware or exploits on unexpected or nonstandard ports are likely to be missed. Additionally, IPS solutions lack the depth of malware detection needed to protect networks — most IPS solutions only look for a few hundred types of common malware — well short of the tens of thousands that exist.

Proxies

Proxy solutions are another means of network traffic control, but here too they look at a limited set of applications or protocols and, as such, only see a partial set of the network traffic that needs to be monitored. By design, proxies need to mimic the applications they are trying to control, so they struggle with updates to existing applications and new applications. As a result, although proxies understand a few protocols in depth, they typically lack the breadth of protocol support needed to control the tunnels and protocols within protocols that hackers use to hide their true traffic. A final issue that plagues proxy solutions is throughput performance caused by the manner in which a proxy terminates an application on the proxy then forwards it on to its destination.

The challenge with any of these network controls is that they do not have the ability to accurately identify applications and malware; they look at only a portion of the traffic and suffer from performance issues.

Security policies must be based on the identity of users and the applications in use — not just on IP addresses, ports, and protocols. Without knowing and controlling exactly who (users) and what (applications and content) have access to the network, enterprise networks may be compromised by applications and malware that can easily bypass port-based network controls.

Crossing Legacy Security Silos

Over the years, enterprises have tried to compensate for the inherent deficiencies in port-based firewalls by implementing a range of supplementary security devices, such as host-based solutions and standalone appliances.

Network versus host-based approaches

Traditionally, enterprises have focused most of their anti-malware time and resources at the end-users' desktops, typically in the form of host antivirus, personal firewalls, and the like. However, as malware evolves from individually infected endpoints to coordinated malware networks, enterprises need to expand their security perspective to incorporate network-level intelligence and controls to complement end-point security measures. Network security has the unique advantage of allowing you to focus on the very trait that distinguishes botnets from earlier forms of malware — its reliance on communication with a larger bot network. To twist John Gage's famous phrase, "the network is the computer," in a very real sense the threat itself has become a network. If your security measures don't operate at this same level, you run a very real risk of missing the forest for the trees.

Additionally, network security mechanisms provide an independent layer of monitoring and control, unlike the endpoints themselves, which can be compromised by malware. Botnets and modern malware can include rootkits that gain root-level access to subvert antivirus protections or other security mechanisms on the target machine. This creates a paradox for the security team, since any security software running on a compromised host cannot truly be trusted. This certainly doesn't imply that host-based security is obsolete, but rather illustrates that blended threats against both the host and the network will likewise demand a security response that leverages the unique strengths of both the host and network security measures.

Integrating multi-disciplinary solutions

Modern malware protection requires an integrated, multi-disciplinary approach to detect malicious traffic, correlate events, and respond accordingly in the enterprise network.

Many organizations have deployed various security solutions in addition to their legacy port-based firewalls, including intrusion prevention systems (IPS), proxy servers, web-content filtering, antivirus gateways, and application-specific solutions — such as instant messaging or e-mail security (anti-spam) appliances — in an effort to shore up their defenses against modern malware threats.

However, this cobbled-together approach to security infra-structure creates problems of its own, including

✔ Not everything that should be inspected is, because these solutions either can't see all of the traffic or rely on the same port- and protocol-based classification scheme as port-based firewalls.

✔ Coverage is only applied to a limited set of traffic, rather than every application.

✔ Policy management, access control rules, and inspection requirements are spread across multiple devices and consoles making it difficult to develop and enforce a con-sistent enterprise security policy.

✔ Performance suffers due to relatively high aggregate latency because the same traffic is scanned and analyzed on multiple devices.

✔ Information is not easily correlated and analyzed between devices, with raw data in multiple different for-mats easily overwhelming security analysts.

More security appliances don't necessarily mean a more secure environment. In fact, the complexity and inconsistency associated with such an approach can actually be a detriment to your organization's security. How? By overwhelming your security team with data from multiple sources that cannot be easily correlated and analyzed.

Chapter 4

What the Next-Generation Firewall Brings to the Fight against Malware

● ●

In This Chapter

▶ Addressing legacy firewall blind spots with a next-generation firewall

▶ Keeping the enterprise safe from malware infections

▶ Finding networked devices that are already infected with malware

● ●

*T*he next-generation firewall provides arguably the most important weapon in the fight against modern malware — the reliable visibility and control of all traffic on the network, irrespective of port or evasive tactics that may be employed. In this chapter, we propose a methodology to limit exposure to malware — as well as to detect and remediate network devices that may already be infected — using the visibility and control capabilities of the next-generation firewall.

Introducing the Next-Generation Firewall

By understanding the full stack behavior of all traffic on the network, you can finely control the behaviors that are allowed in the corporate environment and eliminate the shadows that botnets use to hide. Bots quite simply must talk in order to function. Finding these telltale communications is a critical component of controlling botnets and the threats they pose.

A next-generation firewall performs a true classification of traffic based not simply on port and protocol, but on an ongoing process of application analysis, decryption, decoding, and heuristics as well. These capabilities progressively peel back the layers of a traffic stream to determine its true identity (see Figure 4-1). The ability to pinpoint and analyze even unknown traffic — without regard to port or encryption — is the defining characteristic of a true next-generation firewall and is invaluable in the fight against botnets.

Malware thrives on its ability to blend in with approved or "normal" traffic. The quality of your visibility into that traffic is one of your most critical assets.

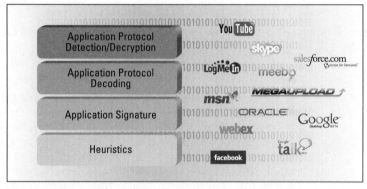

Figure 4-1: Traffic classification in a next-generation firewall.

Additionally, the next-generation firewall provides a fully integrated approach to threat prevention in a unified context: true coordination of multiple security disciplines (for example, application identity, malware detection, intrusion prevention, URL filtering, file type controls, and content inspection), as opposed to simply co-locating them on the same box. This integration provides a far more intelligent and definitive understanding of malware than any individual technology can provide by itself — and is needed in order to see and understand the telltale signs of unknown threats.

Preventing Infection with Next-Generation Firewalls

One of the most important steps that an enterprise can take to control modern malware is to reduce attack vectors and eliminate the ability for bots to hide in the network. Today the majority of vectors used by botnets are virtually unchecked, and botnet traffic is typically small enough that it can easily blend into the background of "normal" network traffic. By regaining full visibility and control of exactly what traffic is allowed into the network and why, security teams can accomplish both of these goals.

Reduce the attack surface

Enforcing positive control is essential to the fight against malware. Positive control greatly reduces the attack surface and mitigates overall risk. Thus, an important first step for the enterprise is to return to a positive control model. Positive control simply means allowing only the specific applications and traffic you want, instead of trying to block everything that you don't want.

Positive control has long been a defining characteristic of network firewalls that separates them from other types of network security devices.

For example, if you want to permit Telnet, you allow TCP port 23 through your firewall. Unfortunately, traditional firewalls cannot properly delineate other applications and protocols that may also be using port 23. Applications and malware now use non-standard, commonly open ports (for example, TCP port 80, 443, and 53) or simply hop between any available open ports to evade traditional firewalls.

Extending positive control to include all applications, irrespective of port, is not as easy as simply flipping a switch. Employees may use certain applications that do not have a readily apparent business value. Additionally, some applications may be used for both personal and business purposes. For example, Facebook can be used for social networking but has also become an increasingly important tool for many company marketing, sales, and recruiting initiatives.

As such, organizational IT security teams should consult appropriate groups and departments within the organization to determine approved applications and uses and to establish appropriate policies. These policies should allow only certain users to access specific applications, or limit the use of specific applications to certain approved features.

To reduce the attack surface, enterprises must

- ✔ Enforce positive control of all network traffic to prevent unnecessary or high-risk traffic, even when encryption or port evasion techniques are used to hide the traffic.

- ✔ Establish policies for approved applications and uses based on business needs and culture, by determining

  - What applications and protocols are in use on the network?

  - What applications are required for the business and who needs to use them?

  - What dual-use or personal applications does the enterprise want to allow?

Control modern malware enabling applications

Applications are an indispensible part of the botnet lifecycle, and are critical to both the initial infection of the target machine and the ongoing command and control of the botnet.

The association between malware and applications is not new. In the past, the de facto enabling application for malware was corporate e-mail. From a security perspective, viruses and e-mail simply went hand-in-hand. Although e-mail is still used by attackers, it has lost some of its luster as e-mail security has become a focal point for many enterprises. Attackers have shifted much of their attention to softer target applications that interact with users in real-time and provide far more threat opportunities. Attackers have gravitated to applications that facilitate social engineering while hiding the presence of a botnet. Social networking and personal use applications meet both of these criteria, and are among the most common sources for malware infection and subsequent command and control of botnets (see Figure 4-2). These applications include social networking, web-based e-mail, instant message (IM), peer-to-peer (P2), and file transfer.

Figure 4-2: Preferred social networking/personal use applications and techniques for modern malware.

These applications are designed to easily share information in a variety of ways, and people often use them with an implied trust and a more cavalier attitude because they may be accustomed to using them outside of the office. This provides an attacker with a multitude of infection opportunities.

Social applications also present an ideal environment for social engineering, enabling an attacker to impersonate a friend or colleague, for example, to lure an unsuspecting victim into clicking a dangerous web link. For all their sophistication, malware infections continue to rely on enticing an unsuspecting user into performing an ill-advised action, such as clicking a malicious link. Instead of opening an e-mail attachment, the click may be a link in a tweet or on a Facebook page that appears to be from a friend. Cross-site scripting can populate dangerous links among friends, and packet sniffing technologies such as FireSheep allow attackers to take over social networking accounts.

Twitter moves to SSL by default

Social networking sites are inadvertently making it easier for malware to remain hidden by moving to the default use of SSL to protect user communications. Twitter has recently joined the ranks of fellow social media giants Facebook and Google by moving to more widespread and default use of SSL to protect their end-users' information. Twitter recently announced that users can set a preference to secure all Twitter communication via HTTPS, which will in time become the default setting for the Twitter service.

This shift to default SSL encryption highlights a very real and important challenge for enterprise security that boils down to this:

✔ Social media applications continue to be the preferred point of infection between enterprise networks and targeted botnets.

✔ Organizations that lack the ability to dynamically look within or enforce security on SSL-encrypted communications are more or less blind to this potentially malicious traffic.

The ramifications for enterprise security are clear: If you can't control social media — and specifically social media that is SSL-encrypted, then you are leaving a clear path open for botnets and malware to get into and out of your network. The shift to SSL by default provides a moderate improvement in privacy for the users, but in the process makes the enterprise far more vulnerable to organized attacks, lost data, and compromised systems.

In their 2010 joint report, *Shadows in the Cloud,* the Information Warfare Monitor (www.infowar-monitor.net) and the Shadowserver Foundation (www.shadowserver.org) provide compelling evidence of the role of social networking applications in the botnet lifecycle. They found that bot-infected machines rarely, if ever, communicate directly with the command-and-control servers. Instead, the initial malware traffic from the infected host would go to popular blogs, Google Groups, Twitter accounts, and Yahoo! Mail accounts, which allowed the malware communications to blend in with "normal" traffic. This illustrates the key lesson that botnets often attempt to blend in with what is considered normal but low-value traffic in the network. How often would you investigate what appears to be an innocuous blog posting?

Control enabling applications by:

✔ Blocking the use of known "bad" applications, such as P2P file-sharing

✔ Limiting application usage to users and groups that have a legitimate and approved business need

✔ Disabling specific features in risky applications, such as file transfers, desktop sharing, and tunneling

✔ Preventing drive-by-downloads from compromised web pages that automatically download malicious files without the user's knowledge

✔ Decrypting SSL traffic selectively, based on application and URL categories (for example, decrypt social networking and webmail, but not financial traffic)

✔ Inspecting and enforcing any risky application traffic that is permitted using a next-generation firewall that provides truly integrated intrusion and threat prevention, malware protection, and URL filtering

Prevent use of circumventors

Common end-user and Web 2.0 applications can be co-opted by malware for use against the enterprise. Equally important, another class of applications are proactively designed to evade traditional network security. These applications include

✔ Remote desktop technologies

✔ Proxies

✔ Purpose-built circumventing applications

Some of these applications have valid business uses, while others are a sure sign of unauthorized and dangerous behavior. In all cases, they require tight control to prevent unmanaged threat vectors into the enterprise.

Remote desktop technologies are popular among end-users and IT support teams. Many web-conferencing applications have added the ability to remotely control a user's machine. Such technologies introduce two important risks:

✔ When a user connects to a remote PC, he is free to surf to any destination and use any application without that traffic being inspected by the firewall. In addition to circumventing policy, the remote desktop opens an unmanaged threat vector by allowing a user to remotely undertake all kinds of risky behavior and then have the results tunneled back to his machine inside the enterprise.

✔ Remote desktop technologies potentially allow an unauthorized user to gain full access to a machine inside the trusted enterprise network. This type of remote control is one of the first objectives of malware, and as such it creates a dangerous opportunity to launch an intrusion. According to Verizon's 2011 Data Breach Investigations Report, 71 percent of breaches and 27 percent of records lost can be attributed to remote access.

Common applications that have valid uses within the enterprise can also create unintentional exposures if improperly used, or used by unauthorized or untrained users. For example, many IT departments use SSH to manage systems and applications in a corporate datacenter. By opening a tunnel into the datacenter, SSH can provide direct, unmanaged access into an enterprise's most critical assets. These applications need to be tightly controlled, limited to approved individuals only, and closely monitored and logged.

Finally, a variety of web proxies and encrypted tunneling applications have been developed to provide secure and anonymous communication across firewalls and other security infrastructure. Proxy technologies such as CGIProxy or PHProxy provide a relatively easy way for users to surf securely without enterprise control and have been found in more than 75 percent of enterprise networks. Applications such as UltraSurf, Hamachi, and Tor are purpose-built to traverse security infrastructures and are regularly updated in order to remain undetected. These applications have very few, if any, valid uses within the enterprise, and their presence generally indicates an attempt to avoid enterprise security. These tools not only pass traffic without being inspected, but they also tend to be used for high-risk behaviors, such as file sharing or accessing expressly blocked content and sites that, in turn, carry a significantly higher risk of malware infection. These applications should be blocked in almost all cases.

Prevent the use of circumventors by:

- ✔ Limiting remote desktop use, for example, to IT support personnel only

- ✔ Securely enabling SSH but preventing SSH tunneling

- ✔ Blocking unapproved proxies and encrypted tunnels, such as UltraSurf and Hamachi

Protect remote users

Traditional enterprise network topologies once maintained a clear perimeter between the inside and outside of the network. However, enterprise computing has evolved to extend well beyond the traditional physical boundaries of the enterprise. Today, users expect to be able to connect to the enterprise network with practically any device — such as a laptop or smartphone — to work literally from anywhere.

This creates a particularly difficult security challenge because the lion's share of an enterprise's security infrastructure and policies are only enforced when the user is inside the physical perimeter of the enterprise network. To make matters worse, a user's behaviors tend to be riskier when outside the office, as they subconsciously revert back to the personal browsing and application habits they use at home. This behavior greatly increases the likelihood of clicking on a dangerous link or visiting a site that serves up a malicious drive-by download.

Protect remote users by:

- ✔ Enforcing full enterprise firewalling and threat prevention, regardless of user location

- ✔ Enabling drive-by-download protections

- ✔ Establishing policies based on user location, such as not allowing remote downloads from secure systems

Investigate unknowns

Once an enterprise has regained positive control and has the ability to inspect and accurately classify approved traffic on its network, it can examine any remaining unknown traffic on the network. Botnets often appear as "unknown" traffic due to their unique behavior and use of proprietary encryption.

Unlike traditional firewalls that typically pass any traffic that uses an approved port, a next-generation firewall provides the ability to find and analyze unknown traffic in the network. Unknown traffic regularly sent by the same client machine should be investigated to determine whether it is being generated by a legitimate application that is not recognized or by a potential malware infection. Security teams can also investigate where the traffic is going:

✔ Does it go out to known malicious websites or to social networking sites?

✔ Does it transmit on a regular schedule?

✔ Does someone attempt to download or upload files to an unknown URL?

Any of these behaviors can indicate the presence of a bot on the client machine. Using a next-generation firewall to accurately identify traffic on the network, "unknown" traffic should become increasingly rare, thus enabling potentially malicious botnet traffic to be quickly found and analyzed.

Increasingly, the next-generation firewall goes beyond analyzing unknown traffic and can even automatically analyze unknown files in a sandbox environment to identify the malicious behaviors of malware. This allows you to focus on unknown files and unknown traffic. Unknowns on the network need to be investigated, identified, and managed. You can quickly and systematically manage unknown traffic by:

✔ Applying a policy on the firewall to block all unknown traffic, or allow and inspect it.

✔ Determining what internal applications exist on the network, and either applying an application override (renaming the traffic) or creating a custom signature.

✔ Analyze unknown or suspicious files in a sandbox to uncover malicious behaviors.

✔ Using packet captures (PCAP) to record the unknown traffic and submit it to your security vendor.

✔ Utilizing behavioral botnet reports and other forensics or reporting tools to determine whether the traffic is a threat.

Investigate "unknown" traffic for potential unauthorized user behavior or botnet activity:

✓ Track source, destination, and volumes of unknown traffic

✓ Correlate against URL, IPS, malware, and file-transfer records

✓ Define custom application IDs for any internal or custom applications, as needed

✓ Deliver packet captures (PCAPs) to your security vendor for further analysis and identification

Finding Infected Hosts with Next-Generation Firewalls

Enterprise machines will inevitably be infected with malware — perhaps through a new type of malware, an unknown vector, or a USB drive. Malware has proven time and again that it is possible to infect even the most heavily secured systems. Thus, it is prudent to assume endpoints are infected and develop the skills necessary to find infected endpoints in the network. This can be a challenging task, given that a bot may have already avoided traditional malware signatures and may already have root-level access on an infected machine.

To pinpoint infected machines, your focus must shift from malware signatures. Instead, you need to analyze unusual or unknown behaviors that are observed on the network. Communication is the Achilles' heel of botnets: they must communicate in order to function, and they must make it difficult to find and trace them. These basic requirements create patterns that can be used to identify bot traffic or behaviors that stand out from the normal network traffic — even if the bot is completely new and unknown.

Find command-and-control traffic

One of the major advantages of a next-generation firewall is its ability to classify potentially complex streams of traffic at the application level. This includes the ability to progressively scan within traffic and peel back protocols running within protocols, until the true underlying application is identified. The ability to identify complex traffic is crucial to detecting the unique command-and-control traffic of botnets. For all intents and purposes, a botnet is an application and its unique traffic can be identified by a true next-generation firewall.

Automate tracking and correlation

The techniques described in the previous sections are crucial, but many organizations don't have the time for manual investigations. A next-generation firewall can automate tracking and correlation with intelligent capabilities including

- ✔ **Unknown TCP/UDP.** Botnet traffic is often encrypted and unknown. Tracking unknown TCP and UDP activity is a great starting point for finding bot-infected machines.

- ✔ **Dynamic DNS (DDNS).** Malware will often use DDNS to bounce traffic between multiple infected hosts with an ever-changing list of IP addresses, making it very difficult to track the true source and destination of a bot.

- ✔ **Known malware sites.** The URL filtering engine of a next-generation firewall constantly tracks sites that have hosted malware whether intentionally or unintentionally.

- ✔ **Recently registered domains.** Botnets often use new domains as they move around to avoid detection and recover. Repeated visits to a newly registered domain are not conclusive, but may be evidence of an infection.

- ✔ **IP addresses instead of domain names.** Bots often use IP addresses, as opposed to normal user (human) browsing that typically prefers friendly URL addresses.

- ✔ **IRC traffic.** IRC traffic is one of the most well-known communication methods for botnets, and provides additional evidence of a bot infection.

Chapter 5

Creating Modern Malware Protection Policies

*F*ar too often, technical solutions are implemented without considering the implications for an organization's overall security strategy. To avoid this mistake, it is important to ensure that your policies are up to date and the technology solutions you are considering support a comprehensive security strategy.

This chapter describes the different types of controls that must be considered in an organization's security policies.

Safe Enablement through Smart Policies

The purpose of enterprise security policies is to reduce the risk of being infected by malware in the first place. But, as discussed in Chapter 1, even the most secure networks with the best security policies are inevitably susceptible to malware and attacks. Likewise, you have to assume that your network will eventually be breached, no matter how well designed your policies are, and plan accordingly. Chapters 3 and 4 cover techniques for detecting and stopping breaches.

Your security policy must help your organization control malware and reduce risks, while also meeting your business requirements. Creating effective security policies requires a keen understanding of the risks posed by the various applications and features used in your network, the business needs of the organization, and your users' work requirements.

IT must play an active role in defining smart policies that enable an organization's users and mitigate risk, but it is important for IT not to be the sole owner of these policies — visible executive support is critical. Adoption of new applications in organizations tends to start from the users themselves, not from policies. But once these applications become integrated into business processes and workflows, rooting them out can be difficult if not impossible to do — even with executive support.

For example, in a heavily regulated environment such as stock trading, the use of instant messaging may be subject to retention and auditability rules. IT's role is to educate the traders on the security risks of instant messaging tools, participate in the development of the acceptable use policy (AUP), and subsequently monitor and enforce its use. In this example, that policy could prevent the traders from using Facebook and MSN chat for instant messaging, but enable an internal chat server instead.

Governance and management work best if they are based on a set of smart corporate policies that are developed by the four major stakeholders in the enterprise network landscape: IT, HR, executive management, and the users. Clearly IT has a role to play, but it can't be the strictly defined role that it often plays. Neither can IT be lax about its role as the enabler and governor of applications and technology.

Application controls

Enablement is about knowing and understanding users and their behaviors, and applications and their associated risks. In the case of popular applications (such as social media), the users have long since decided on the benefits — and are, far too often, oblivious to the threats and risks. As a result, it's vital to match users' needs with the most appropriate applications and features, while also educating users about the implicit risks of those applications and features.

Enabling Facebook usage while protecting the business

Facebook is rapidly extending its influence from the personal world to the corporate world, since employees now use these applications to get their jobs done. At the same time, many organizations are looking at the nearly 600 million Facebook users as an opportunity to conduct research, execute targeted marketing, gather product feedback, and increase awareness. The end result is that Facebook can help organizations improve their bottom line.

However, formally enabling the use of Facebook introduces several challenges to organizations. Many organizations are unaware of how heavily Facebook is being used, or for what purpose. In most cases, policies governing specific usage are nonexistent or unenforceable. Finally, users tend to be too trusting, operating in a "click now, think later" mentality that introduces significant security risks.

Like any application that is brought into the enterprise by end-users, blindly allowing Facebook usage may result in propagation of threats, loss of data, and damage to the corporate reputation. Blindly blocking Facebook usage is also an inappropriate response because it may play an important role in the business and may force users to find alternative means of accessing it (such as proxies, circumvention tools, and others).

Organizations should follow a systematic process to develop, enable, and enforce appropriate Facebook usage policies while simultaneously protecting network resources.

1. **Find out who's using Facebook.** There are many cases in which a "corporate" Facebook presence may already be established by marketing or sales, so it is critical that IT determine which social networking applications are in use, who is using them, and the associated business objectives. By meeting with the business groups and discussing the common company goals, IT can use this step to move away from the image of "always saying no" and towards the role of business enabler.

2. **Develop a corporate Facebook policy.** Once Facebook usage patterns are determined, organizations should engage in discussions regarding what should and should not be said or posted about the company, the competition, and the appropriate language. Educating users on the security risks associated with Facebook is another important element to consider when encouraging usage for business purposes. With a "click first, think later" mentality, Facebook

(continued)

(continued)

users tend to place too much trust in their network of friends, potentially introducing malware while placing personal and corporate data at risk.

3. **Use technology to monitor and enforce policy.** The outcome of each of these policy discussions should be documented with an explanation of how IT will apply security policies to safely and securely enable use of Facebook within enterprise environments.

As Facebook moves to SSL encryption, enterprises should strongly consider decrypting traffic to and from Facebook.

Documenting and enforcing a social networking usage policy can help organizations improve their bottom line while boosting employee morale. An added benefit is that it can help bridge the chasm that commonly exists between the IT department and business groups.

Application enablement typically includes restricting the use of unneeded high-risk applications while managing allowed applications to reduce the inherent risks they may bring with them. Establishing effective policies requires open dialogue among users, IT, and management to truly understand which applications have legitimate business uses and value. Certain applications are known to be conduits for malware, both in terms of infection and ongoing command and control. Peer-to-peer applications, such as BitTorrent, are iconic examples.

On the other hand, many applications are not definitively good or bad (black or white), and will instead land in a gray area of enterprise security policy. These applications may have business value but can also carry considerable risk. Safe enablement should be the goal for these applications. In this case, applications can be allowed but constrained to only allow needed features while blocking higher risk features. For example, an enterprise may enable a web meeting application, but not allow the remote desktop capability that could allow a remote attacker to take control of a machine. Enabling policies could also limit certain applications or features to specific approved users, or could scan the application to ensure that no unapproved files or content is being transferred. The ultimate goal is to attack the risk in the application, not the application itself.

Application controls should be part of the overarching corporate security policy. As part of the process of implementing an application control policy, IT should make a concerted effort to learn about new and evolving Web 2.0 applications. This includes embracing them for all their intended purposes and, if needed, proactively installing them or enabling them in a lab environment to see how they act. Peer discussions, message boards, blogs, and developer communities are also valuable sources of information.

User controls

Most companies have some type of application usage policy, outlining which applications are allowed and which are prohibited. Every employee is expected to understand the contents of this application usage policy and the ramifications of not complying with it, but there are a number of unanswered questions, including

- ✔ Given the ever-growing numbers and types of applications, how will an employee know which applications are allowed and which are prohibited?
- ✔ How is the list of unapproved applications updated, and who ensures employees know the list has changed?
- ✔ What constitutes a policy violation?
- ✔ What are the ramifications of policy violations — a reprimand or termination of employment?

The development of policy guidelines is often a challenging and polarizing process. Determining what should be allowed and what should be prohibited while balancing risk and reward elicits strong opinions from all the major stakeholders.

Further complicating the process is the fact that new applications and technologies are often adopted within an organization long before appropriate policies governing their safe and appropriate use are ever considered or developed.

Documented employee policies need to be a key piece of the application control puzzle, but employee controls as a stand-alone mechanism will remain largely ineffective for safe enablement of new and evolving applications.

Network controls

Given that modern malware most often uses the network for infection and ongoing command and control, the network is an obvious and critical policy-enforcement point. With application-enablement policies in place, IT can shift its attention to inspecting the content of allowed traffic. This inspection often includes looking at traffic for known malware, command-and-control patterns, exploits, dangerous URLs, and dangerous or risky file types. When possible, policies that focus on the content of traffic should be coordinated as part of a single unified policy, where the rules (and the results of those rules) can all be seen in context. If content policies are spread across multiple solutions, modules, or monitors, piecing together a coordinated logical enforcement policy becomes increasingly difficult for IT security staff. Understanding whether these policies are working once they are implemented will likewise be difficult.

The goal should be to create written policies that reflect the policies' intentions just like someone might describe them orally. For example, "only allow designated employees to use SharePoint, inspect all SharePoint traffic for exploits and malware, disallow the transfer of files types X, Y, and Z, and look for the word *confidential* in traffic going to untrusted zones."

Another key component of network policies is the absolute need to retain visibility into the traffic content. SSL is increasingly used to secure traffic destined for the Internet. Although this may provide privacy for that particular session, if IT lacks the ability to look inside the SSL tunnel, SSL can also provide an opaque tunnel within which malware can be introduced into the network environment. IT must balance the need to look within SSL against both privacy requirements for end-users and the overall performance requirements of the network. For this reason, it is important to establish SSL decryption policies that can be enforced selectively by application and URL category. For example, social media traffic could be decrypted and inspected for malware, while traffic to financial or healthcare sites is left encrypted.

Endpoint controls

The end-user's machine is the most common target for modern malware and is a critical point for policy enforcement. Endpoint policies must incorporate ways of ensuring that antivirus and various host-based security solutions are properly installed and up to date.

Although targeted attacks are becoming more common, the majority of threats today continue to be known threats with known signatures. Gartner, Inc. predicts that known threats will comprise 95 percent of all threats through 2015. As such, these endpoint solutions must be kept up to date and must be audited regularly.

Similarly, you need to have a method for validating that host operating systems are patched and up to date. Many malware infections begin with a remote exploit that targets a known vulnerability in the operating system or application. Thus, keeping these components up to date is a critical aspect of reducing the attack surface of the enterprise.

As with employee policies, desktop controls are a key piece to the safe enablement of applications in the enterprise. Desktop controls present IT departments with significant challenges. Careful consideration should be applied to the granularity of the desktop controls and the impact on employee productivity. The drastic step of desktop lockdown to keep users from installing their own applications is a task that is easier said than done *and*, if used alone, will be ineffective. Here's why:

- ✔ Remotely connected laptops, Internet downloads, USB drives, and e-mail are all means of installing applications that may or may not be allowed on the network.

- ✔ Completely removing administrative rights is difficult to implement and, in some cases, severely limits end-user capabilities to an unacceptable level.

- ✔ USB drives are now capable of running applications, so a Web 2.0 application, for example, can be accessed after network admission is granted.

Desktop controls can complement documented employee policies as a means to safely enable Web 2.0 applications.

Addressing Mobile and Remote Users

That the modern enterprise has and continues to become far more distributed than in the past is no secret. Users simply expect to be able to connect and work from any location, whether at an airport, a coffee shop, a hotel room, or at home. This change means that more and more workers and data may be beyond the physical perimeter of the enterprise, and thus also beyond the protections of traditional perimeter security solutions. The key is to build a security architecture that doesn't treat these mobile or remote users as exceptions; they need the same application, user, and content protections when they are outside the perimeter that they would receive when they are inside.

Building consistency into the architecture of the network requires careful planning and is a must for any security policy to address the realities of modern computing.

Similarly, security policies must address the use of endpoint devices other than standard corporate-issued equipment. Users working from home may use their own personal computers, which are increasingly as likely to be running Apple OSX as they are to be running Windows. Other devices used to remotely connect to enterprise networks include smartphones, tablets, and iOS devices, such as iPhones and iPads. All of these devices must also be addressed in order to prevent blind spots in your organization's security policies.

Mobile malware is still in its infancy, but it does exist and is likely to become a major threat in the near future. As mobile devices grow more powerful, they will increasingly be used as a replacement for the PC, storing vast amounts of personal — and valuable — data that is largely unprotected.

Chapter 6

Ten Best Practices for Controlling Modern Malware

*I*n this chapter, we recommend ten best practices to control modern malware and botnets. These recommenda-
tions are not intended to replace, but rather to supplement,
the existing security strategies of your organization, as part of
a modern coordinated approach to defense in depth.

Ensure Visibility into All Traffic

You can't control what you can't see. Modern malware is specifically designed to evade legacy port-based firewalls that
allow or block traffic based on known TCP and UDP ports.
Ensure visibility into all traffic on the enterprise network by:

   ✔ Accurately classifying all traffic.

   • Legacy port-based firewalls that simply match
     common TCP and UDP ports to a standard proto-
     col are easily bypassed by malware and evasive
     applications.

   • A next-generation firewall uses protocol decoders
     to fully analyze the application layer and to accu-
     rately classify the application and traffic.

✔ Extending visibility beyond the perimeter.

- Segment the network internally. Protect high-value targets such as domain controllers and e-mail and database servers, with logical network segmentation (when practical) and special security policies that identify suspicious activity (such as excessive nmap lookups and database queries).

- Protect remote users. Deliver the same level of application control, threat prevention, and policy enforcement for remote users and mobile devices outside the network perimeter as for those inside.

Restrict High-Risk Applications

The number and diversity of applications in the enterprise has exploded, and almost all of them can introduce some level of risk. Although some of these applications may have legitimate use cases, their presence within an enterprise network can introduce a great deal of unnecessary risk into the network. Most applications are designed for easy use, easy sharing, and easy interaction. Security is almost always an afterthought, and it is up to IT security teams to control these risks.

Consumerization occurs as users increasingly find personal technology and applications that are more powerful or capable, more convenient, less expensive, quicker to install, and easier to use than corporate IT solutions. According to Gartner, Inc., consumerization will be the most significant trend affecting IT through 2015. Organizations should control the risk introduced by applications by restricting the use of high-risk applications. Here's how:

✔ Block (or limit) P2P applications

✔ Block unneeded applications that can tunnel other applications

✔ Block applications known to be used by malware

✔ Block anonymizers (such as Tor)

✔ Block encrypted tunnel applications (such as UltraSurf)

✔ Limit use of approved proxies to authorized users with a legitimate business need

✔ Limit use of remote desktop protocols and applications to authorized users with a legitimate business need (such as IT support personnel)

Selectively Decrypt and Inspect SSL Traffic

Recent analysis of live enterprise networks shows that the reach of SSL is exploding, with roughly 36 percent of total enterprise bandwidth being consumed by applications that can run SSL or hop ports (see Figure 6-1).

SSL Application Bandwidth Consumption (Worldwide)

SSL: 443 Only, 14%

SSL: 443 or other port, 8%

All Other Applications, 77%

SSL: Any Port but 443, 1%

Source: Palo Alto Networks, Application Usage and Risk Report, May 2011

Figure 6-1: SSL application bandwidth consumption (worldwide).

While SSL certainly provides security for the individual session, it can also create a problem for enterprise security by obscuring the traffic from network security solutions such as intrusion prevention systems (IPS), anti-malware, and data loss prevention (DLP) solutions. To make matters worse, the very sites and applications that are adopting SSL are the same ones that hackers favor for launching and maintaining their ongoing attacks.

IT and security teams should implement best practices and policies to selectively identify, decrypt, and inspect high-risk SSL traffic while maintaining an appropriate balance of performance. Enterprises need to control SSL traffic with:

- ✔ **Decrypt policies** that allow decryption and inspection of the following SSL traffic:

  - Social networking

  - Web-based e-mail

  - Instant messaging

  - Message boards

  - Microblogging

  - Gaming sites

- ✔ **Do-not-decrypt policies** that protect the confidentiality and integrity of the following SSL traffic:

  - Health care applications, information, and sites

  - Financial applications, data, and sites

  - Secure channels

Sandbox Unknown Executables and Attachments

Modern attackers are increasingly turning to customized malware targeted at a particular enterprise network or a specific host. This strategy makes the malware extremely unique and almost certainly enables it to pass through security measures without triggering known malware signatures. This trend highlights one of the limitations in traditional anti-malware security that has existed for years: Signatures can only protect against malware that has been previously detected and analyzed. This reactive approach creates a window of opportunity for malware (the time that new malware is "in the wild") in which enterprises are not protected and vulnerable to attack.

To address this vulnerability, enterprises should supplement their signature-based tools with direct analysis of unknown executables for malicious behaviors. Direct analysis is typically done by placing the unknown executable file in a virtual environment to observe how it would behave in a vulnerable environment. This approach can expose some of the tell-tale signs of malware — such as altering operating system files, making changes to registry settings, or injecting themselves into other running processes — and provides IT security teams with a method for definitively identifying malware even when it is not recognized by signature-based anti-malware solutions.

IT security teams should have the ability to create signatures on demand when new malware is identified, and distribute these custom signatures to all of the organization's network gateways in order to protect against new malware threats. It's not enough to simply put a sandbox into your lab. You must build in the ability to quickly and centrally determine whether a given file has already been analyzed, and then quickly deliver protections to all ingress/egress points when a malicious file is detected.

Block URLs That Are Known to Host Malware

Even completely valid websites can be compromised and serve up malware to unsuspecting visitors. However, some sites are clearly more dangerous than others, and a strong URL filtering solution should be able to keep track of sites that have been known to deliver malware. This approach, much like anti-malware and intrusion prevention signature-based solutions, requires constant diligence by the security vendor to keep updated. IT security teams need to challenge their vendors to ensure that URL lists are properly maintained and automatically updated.

In addition to known bad sites and URLs, extra caution should be exercised with any recently registered or unclassified domains. Botnets and malware move quickly between such new sites in order to avoid detection and to cover their tracks.

IT security teams must be able to update URL classifications based on malware that may have been identified through sandboxing. An important benefit of a malware sandbox is the ability to see how and where the malware came from — and where it connects back to. This will allow security teams to immediately update the lists of dangerous URLs, based on actual threats observed in the network.

Enforce Drive-by-Download Protection

Infection via drive-by-downloads has become a very common method for malware delivery. A drive-by-download occurs when a user unknowingly visits a malicious or compromised website that automatically downloads software to the user's computer without the person's knowledge or permission. The host browser and operating system fails to detect or report the download and installation, leaving the user's machine vulnerable to infection.

Enterprises must enforce drive-by-download protection to prevent infections by:

- ✔ Detecting downloads in the background, even unknown exploits and malware

- ✔ Automatically reporting drive-by-downloads to the user and either blocking the download or requiring the user to acknowledge and permit the download

- ✔ Training users not to just click "OK" or "Accept" but to read and understand pop-up warnings from their network firewall

Block Known Exploits and Malware

Although this may seem obvious, known threats (as opposed to new and evolving unknown threats or threats "in the wild") still constitute the majority of threats leading to successful malware infections and attacks against the enterprise today. Malware and exploit kits are increasingly popular and have supercharged the malware economy.

Gartner, Inc., estimates that through 2015, more than 90 percent of malware and exploits will continue to be known threats.

IT organizations commonly disable many known vulnerability signatures and features (such as real-time vulnerability scanning) in intrusion prevention systems or anti-malware software for performance reasons. The single unified threat engine in a true next-generation firewall is designed to process high volumes of network traffic in real-time to detect all threats, without sacrificing performance or reliability.

Limit Traffic for Common Applications to Default Ports

Certain ports practically have to be open on a firewall for an enterprise network to function. For example, most web browsing requires TCP ports 53 (DNS), 80 (HTTP), and 443 (HTTPS), and e-mail communication requires TCP port 25 (SMTP). Attackers take advantage of this requirement with botnets and malware that regularly communicate on ports that are almost always open by default.

Legacy port-based firewalls simply allow traffic across an open port and assume that it is the default application or protocol for that port. A next-generation firewall compares the traffic to application signatures in order to accurately identify the application or protocol, and allows you to set policies that permit only the default application on a common port and block everything else.

Evaluate Network and Application Events in Context

It is important to understand that application signatures, network behaviors, and malware sources are all interrelated, and need to be correlated and evaluated in context. Traditional security infrastructures that provide "defense in depth" through separate devices such as port-based firewalls, intrusion prevention, web-content filtering, and anti-malware software can overwhelm security teams with data that cannot be easily correlated. A true solution should help you to make intelligent security decisions based on context, rather than just hoping for a "silver bullet" against a specific threat.

To evaluate events in context:

- ✔ Develop context-based visibility with accurate information about applications, signatures, sources, and behaviors
- ✔ Correlate events by user and application, including
  - Known malware
  - Known exploits
  - Phone-home detection
  - Download history
  - URL categories

Investigate Unknowns

A true next-generation firewall accurately classifies all known traffic and allows you to create customized classifications for any remaining unknowns, such as internal or custom-developed applications. Unknown traffic should be tracked and investigated to find potential malware or other unidentified threats on the enterprise network. In addition to unknown traffic, you should investigate

- ✔ **Unknown or unclassified URLs.** Unknown or recently registered URLs are significant because malware and bot-herders regularly rotate between URLs that are used for command and control to impede discovery and take-down efforts. Unknown traffic going to unknown URL categories should be treated as highly suspicious.

- ✔ **Unknown encryption.** Customized encryption is often used by malware to hide their communications. Use the capabilities of a true next-generation firewall to inspect encrypted traffic and to ensure that all traffic on the network has a known, legitimate purpose.

Glossary

adware: Pop-up advertising programs that are commonly installed with freeware or shareware.

APT: Advanced Persistent Threat. An Internet-borne attack usually perpetrated by a group of individuals with significant resources, such as organized crime or a rogue nation-state.

backdoor: Malware that enables an attacker to bypass normal authentication to gain access to a compromised system.

BitTorrent: A P2P file-sharing communications protocol that distributes large amounts of data widely without the original distributor incurring the costs of hardware, hosting, and bandwidth resources.

bootkit: A kernel-mode variant of a rootkit, commonly used to attack computers that are protected by full-disk encryption.

bot: A target machine that is infected by malware and is part of a botnet (also known as a zombie).

bot-herder: The owner or individual that controls a botnet.

botnet: A broad network of bots working together.

DDNS: Dynamic DNS is a technique used to update domain name system (DNS) records for networked devices in real time.

DDoS: Distributed denial-of-service is a large-scale attack that typically uses bots in a botnet to crash a targeted network or server.

drive-by-download: Software, often malware, downloaded onto a computer from the Internet without the user's knowledge or permission.

IPsec: An open-standard protocol used for secure VPN communications over public IP-based networks.

IRC: Internet Relay Chat.

malware: Malicious software or code that typically damages or disables, takes control of, or steals information from a computer system. Broadly includes viruses, worms, Trojan horses, logic bombs, rootkits, bootkits, backdoors, spyware, and adware.

MBR: Master Boot Record.

Next-generation firewall (NGFW): A firewall beyond traditional port-based controls that enforces policy based on application, user, and content regardless of port or protocol.

Nmap: Network mapper is a security scanner used to discover network hosts and services.

PCAP: Packet capture.

RDP: Remote Desktop Protocol.

rootkit: Malware that provides privileged (root-level) access to a computer.

SMTP: Simple Mail Transfer Protocol.

spear phishing: A targeted phishing attempt that seems more credible to its victims and thus has a higher probability of success. For example, a spear phishing e-mail may spoof an organization or individual that the recipient actually knows.

SSH: Secure Shell is a set of standards and an associated network protocol that establishes a secure channel between a local and a remote computer.

SSL: Secure Sockets Layer is a transport layer protocol that provides session-based encryption and authentication for secure communication between clients and servers.

SYN: TCP synchronization bit.

TCP: Transmission Control Protocol.

UDP: User Datagram Protocol.

Web widget: A small application that an end user can install and run within a web page.